WAITING ALLIGATORS

by William Muñoz

Lerner Publications Company • Minneapolis

Website address: www.lernerbooks.com

Curriculum Development Director: Nancy M. Campbell

Words in *italic type* are explained in a glossary
on page 30.

Library of Congress Cataloging-in-Publication Data

Muñoz, William.
    Waiting alligators / William Muñoz.
      p. cm. — (Pull ahead books)
    Includes index.
    Summary: Simple text and photographs present
the characteristics, habitats, behavior, and life cycle
of the American alligator.
    ISBN 0-8225-3615-3 (hc. : alk. paper). —
    ISBN 0-8225-3621-8 (pbk. : alk. paper)
    1. American alligator—Juvenile literature.
[1. Alligators.] I. Title. II. Series.
QL666.C925M85 1999
597.98—dc21   98–27339

Manufactured in the United States of America
1 2 3 4 5 6 – JR – 04 03 02 01 00 99

What is this thing floating quietly
in the water? Is it a log?

Surprise! This is an animal called an alligator.

Alligators spend a lot of time waiting quietly. Do you know why?

Alligators wait for food
to come near them.

They eat turtles, fish, birds, and
other animals that come near.

Alligators have strong jaws
and sharp teeth.

Their jaws and teeth help them
catch animals.

An alligator turns its head
sideways to bite an animal.

Then the alligator shakes
the animal back and forth.

An alligator cannot swallow
the same way you do.

It must lift its head to let
food fall down its throat.

Alligators usually wait for food,
but they can chase animals, too.

How fast do you think
alligators can move?

Alligators have short legs, but they can run as fast as humans.

Alligators can run fast for only a few seconds.

Alligators can swim very fast
and very far.

Their strong tails push them
through the water.

What else do you think
strong tails are good for?

Alligators use their tails to dig big holes called *gator holes.*

Gator holes fill with water even in hot, dry weather.

Animals come to eat and drink
at gator holes.

These animals are food
for alligators.

When it is too hot outside,
alligators cool down in gator holes.

Alligators are *ectotherms.*

Their body heat changes to match the warmth or cold around them.

When an alligator feels too cold,
it lies in the sun.

The sun warms up its body.

The body of an alligator
is covered with *scales.*

Scales are part of the skin.
They are strong like fingernails.

Because alligators are ectotherms with short legs and scales,

they belong to a group of animals called *reptiles*.

Like most reptiles, alligators have babies that come from eggs.

Female alligators lay the eggs. Can you guess where?

Females bury their eggs in nests they make from mud and plants.

As the plants rot, they make heat to keep the eggs warm.

This alligator is guarding
her nest.

What do you think she will do
if an animal comes too near?

HISS! She tells the animal
to go away.

Then she chases it away.

After waiting about 65 days, the female hears sounds in the nest.

Her babies are peeping as they *hatch* from the eggs!

She digs up the eggs to help
her babies out of the nest.

She leads the babies to water.
They will be safer there.

Baby alligators stay with their
mother for about one year.

She shows them how to catch food and stay safe,

while they wait until they grow big and can live on their own.

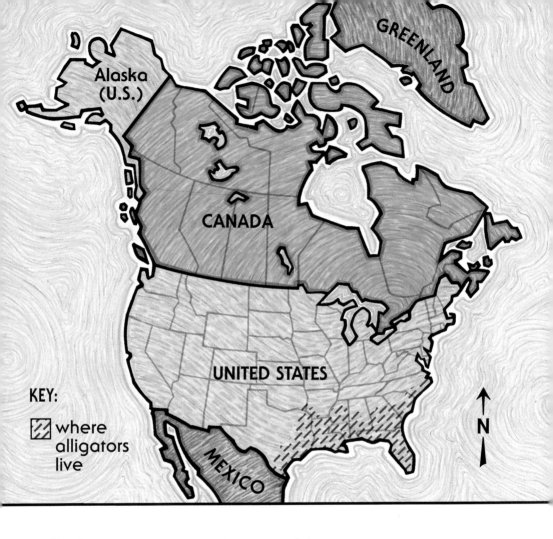

Find your state or province on this map.
Do alligators live near you?

Parts of an Alligator's Body

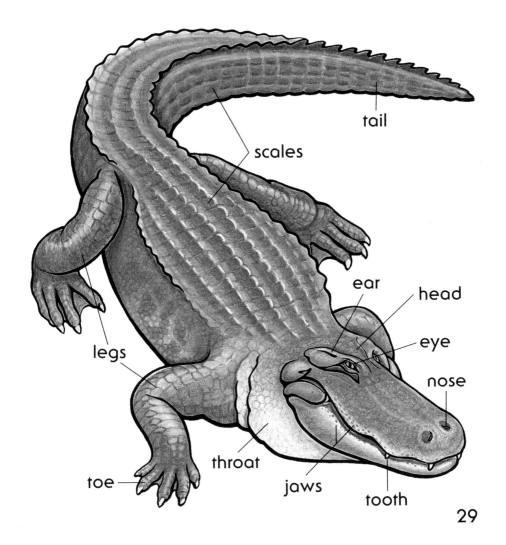

tail

scales

ear

head

eye

nose

legs

throat

toe

jaws

tooth

Glossary

ectotherms: animals whose body heat changes to match the warmth or cold around them

gator holes: big, water-filled holes dug by alligators

hatch: come out

reptiles: crawling or creeping animals that usually have scales. A reptile's body heat changes to match the warmth or cold around it. (Snakes, alligators, lizards, and turtles are reptiles.)

scales: a reptile's strong, waterproof body covering

Hunt and Find

- **baby alligators** on pages 24–26
- alligators **eating** on pages 7–8, 31
- an alligator **floating** on page 3
- **food animals** for alligators on pages 5, 14
- **nests** of alligators on pages 21–23

The publisher wishes to extend special thanks to our **series consultant,** Sharyn Fenwick. An elementary science-math specialist, Mrs. Fenwick was the recipient of the National Science Teachers Association 1991 Distinguished Teaching Award. In 1992, representing the state of Minnesota at the elementary level, she received the Presidential Award for Excellence in Math and Science Teaching.

Sandy Muñoz

About the Author

William Muñoz both wrote about and photographed the alligators in this book. He has worked as a nature photographer for over 20 years. You can see his pictures of animals and plants in many books for children. Some of these books are *Watchful Wolves, Ants, Apple Trees,* and *Polar Bears* (Lerner Publications) and *Horses, Dogs,* and *Cattle* (Carolrhoda Books). William lives with his wife and son in Missoula, Montana.